Should Do
in *Her*
Lifetime

98 Things a Woman Should Do in Her Lifetime

Rebekah Shardy

**Andrews McMeel
Publishing, LLC**

Kansas City

98 Things a Woman Should Do in Her Lifetime copyright © 2003 by Rebekah Shardy. All rights reserved. Printed in China. No part of this book may be used or reproduced in any manner whatsoever without written permission except in the case of reprints in the context of reviews. For information, write Andrews McMeel Publishing, LLC, an Andrews McMeel Universal company, 4520 Main Street, Kansas City, Missouri 64111.

This book developed out of an article originally published in the December 9, 1999, issue of the *Colorado Springs Independent*.

ISBN-13: 987-0-7407-3338-3
ISBN-10: 0-7407-3338-9

Library of Congress Control Number: 2002111566

08 09 10 WKT 20 19 18 17 16 15 14 13 12 11

——— ATTENTION: SCHOOLS AND BUSINESSES ———

Andrews McMeel books are available at quantity discounts with bulk purchase for educational, business, or sales promotional use. For information, please write to: Special Sales Department, Andrews McMeel Publishing, LLC, 4520 Main Street, Kansas City Missouri 64111.

To my mother's death-defying
heart, which knew how to soar
above a world of limitations,
and to my mentor and muse,
Iris Trachsel, who taught me
to never look down when you're
crossing the highwire of life.

...1...

Allow your chewy,
salty heart
to be marinated
in the tender juices
of a younger
man's obsession.

Run for office, win, and then resign in a grand gesture of moral indigestion.

...3...

Ride a train
through Europe
(better yet,
the Orient Express).

...4...

Say grace to
the Goddess.

...5...

Vote from lust.

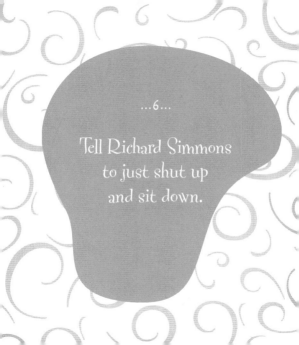

...6...

Tell Richard Simmons
to just shut up
and sit down.

...7...

Paint a mural
of your
imagined
past lives.

...8...

Buy a pair of castanets
and learn to use them.

...9...

Sing to a child.

...10...

Sing to a
dying parent.

Order a whole Peking duck
when dining out alone.

Cultivate savoir faire—
an effortless knack for
saying or doing just the
right thing in any situation.

...13...

Go a month without
shaving your legs.

...14...

Buy a really expensive,
well-made pair of boots.

...15...

Write your
own erotica.

If you're lucky,
learn to do one good impression,
say, of Clint Eastwood;
well, *do you feel lucky,* punk?

...17...

Release one
grudge a month.

...18...

Organize a day spa
for women living at a
domestic violence shelter
with services donated from
a local beauty school.

...19...

Audition for
community
theater.

...20...

Get published.

...21...

Teach someone,
besides a child,
to read.

...22...

Invent a punch that will
raise eyebrows and
lower inhibitions.

Don't indulge in one
judgmental thought
for an entire day.
Okay, an hour.

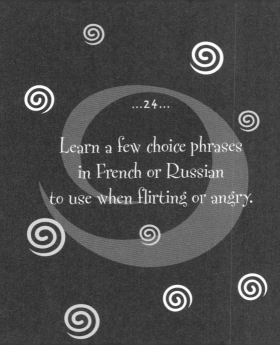

...24...

Learn a few choice phrases
in French or Russian
to use when flirting or angry.

...25...

Stay in a convent for a week.

Ride a motorcycle
alone across the
Nevada desert.

...27...

Make wine from
dandelions growing in
your backyard and send
it to the CEO of
Greener Chemical Lawns, Inc.

...28...

Start a wild rumor
that something wonderful
will happen later this year.

Squeeze a cute
fireman
because it's
"Public Hero
Appreciation Day."

...30...

Learn to belly dance
and integrate it into
your lovemaking.

Apply for a scholarship
to an art, literary, or
spiritual retreat
that intrigues you.

Design a picnic around
aphrodisiacs—raw oysters,
champagne, rose petal jam
on chocolate fingers—
then whisper in another's
ear the sensual images
that passing clouds suggest.

···33···

Be someone's
fairy godmother.
Wand optional.

...34...

Write an unauthorized
biography of your family,
including embarrassing
photos, a tribute to the
infamous black sheep,
and favorite recipes.

...35...

Serve
something
flambé.

On the hottest day in
August donate matinee
tickets to a movie in
an air-conditioned
theater to kids
living in a
homeless shelter.

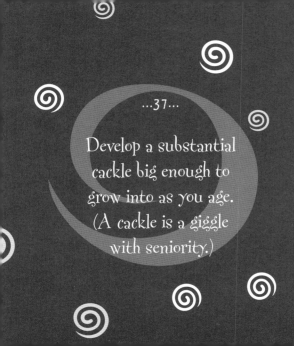

...37...

Develop a substantial
cackle big enough to
grow into as you age.
(A cackle is a giggle
with seniority.)

...38...

Flirt with a stewardess
just for the hell of it.
(It's nicer than air rage.)

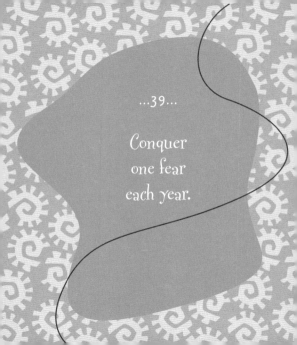

...39...

Conquer
one fear
each year.

Play the sax or cello
or learn at least one
aria or gospel song.

...41...

Interview three
plastic surgeons
and tell them why
your body's flaws
are precious to you.

Refuse to settle down.

...43...

Wear a fedora
in public.

...44...

Tell only the
truth to a child.

Tell the waitress at
Denny's that the lines on
her palm indicate she is
destined for greatness.

...46...

Whisper your
darkest secrets
to a beloved tree.

...47...

Let someone make love
to you in a fragrant field
of sweet grass
at dusk in
late summer.

...48...

Invite an old rival
to tea and talk frankly
about the past
and the present.

...49...

Learn to recognize
at least one constellation
year-round.

...50...

Rent a luxury hotel
room for a night alone.

Bring fried chicken
and potato salad to the
exhausted ER crew
that has to work on
the Fourth of July.

...52...

Adopt a hairstyle
you know everyone
will hate but that
you like anyway.

...53...

Grow at least three
Victorian flowers—
like peonies, phlox,
and foxglove—
to make a lovely nosegay.

Look up the definition
of "nosegay" and use
it in a sentence.

Learn the names and
at least one tradition of the
Native Americans that originally
lived near your home.

...56...

Make friends with
silence and solitude
without having to
get sick first.

...57...

Write a love letter that
you know has the power to
change someone's life.

Burn a CD with music
you want played at your
wake or funeral;
baffle generations to come
by including the rap song
"I Like Big Butts."

Cry in the rain.

...60...

Accept your
luminous,
inimitable
talents.

...61...

Rent a car for
an hour at the
local racetrack.

Remember life is
too short for ironing,
nonfat dairy creamer,
and regret of any kind.

...63...

Learn how to
make a decadent
chocolate mousse
with tofu.

...64...

Write an autobiography
about the life
you didn't choose.

...65...

Smuggle good scotch
to your (or someone else's)
dad in the nursing home.

...66...

Start a
food fight.

Showcase a hobby
you feel passionate
about on public access
cable television.

Practice telepathy
with your cat.

...69...

Change one thing
about your life
that you've accepted.

...70...

Accept one thing
about your life that
you've tried to change.

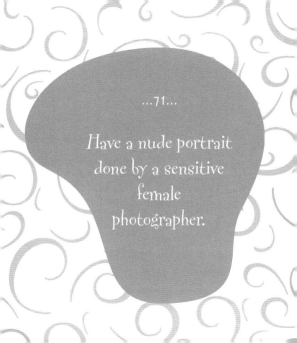

...71...

Have a nude portrait done by a sensitive female photographer.

...72...

Go gray
for a month.

Dance under a
full moon with a gaggle
of cackling women.

Read a book on
astrophysics or
molecular biology
from cover to cover.

...75...

Realize you are not
merely your body.

Create a comfort station at work
or home stocked with things you love:
Jujubes, cucumber hand cream,
cherry blossom tea,
a special letter or picture.

...77...

Create an altar
in honor of your
female ancestors
and mentors.

Write three haiku poems
about your most amazing,
horrible, and baffling
sexual experiences and
frame them for your boudoir.

...79...

Be the boss of
someone who is
bigger and has a
deeper voice than you.

...80...

Rent a
tuxedo.

...81...

Explore your inner pagan
by creating your own
seasonal rituals:

...82...

At the spring equinox,
detox with a juice fast,
sauna, and deep
muscle massage.

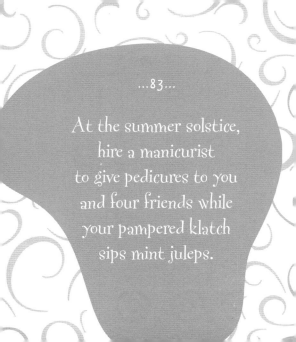

...83...

At the summer solstice,
hire a manicurist
to give pedicures to you
and four friends while
your pampered klatch
sips mint juleps.

At the fall equinox,
organize a black-clad,
beatnik poetry reading
with the themes of rain,
dissolution, and romance.

...85...

At the winter solstice,
plant a circle of globed candles
in a snowdrift and
make wishes every night
until they burn out.

Do Stevie Nicks
on karaoke—sober.

...87...

Read James Joyce
to telemarketers.

...88...

Stick your nose
where it doesn't belong
to stop child or
animal abuse.

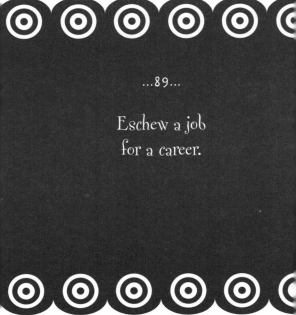

...89...

Eschew a job
for a career.

...90...

Eschew a career
for a life.

...91...

Buy one
significant
piece of
original art.

...92...

Kiss a girl.

Lead a protest or
commit an act of
civil disobedience.

Forgive
the unforgivable.

...95...

Embrace
change.

...96...

Drop cable to spend the money on a $50 bottle of champagne each month.

...97...

Abandon
self-doubt.

Give birth to your
heart's deepest desire
and develop postnatal
amnesia about the pain
so you can do it again.